1990

THE ART OF BLACK AFRICA

© 1985 Ediciones Polígrafa, S. A.
Balmes, 54 - 08007 Barcelona (Spain)

Translation by Dr. Ann Keep

I.S.B.N.: 84-343-0448-1
Dep. Leg.: B. 37046 - 1985 (Printed in Spain)

Printed in Spain by La Polígrafa, S. A.
Parets del Vallès (Barcelona)

Elsy Leuzinger

THE ART OF BLACK AFRICA

Photographs by
Isabelle Wettstein & Brigitte Kauf

EDICIONES POLIGRAFA, S. A.

African art is rooted in religion. This does not mean that Africans would be so presumptuous as to make images of the great creator-god. It is rather the case that they try to put the divine power, the eternal vital force which suffuses creation, into a form that befits it, thereby ensuring its favourable disposition and enlisting its aid and protection. African works of art — masks, sculptures and other ritual implements — are nothing less than media designed for a supernatural power. They have to be fashioned with such beauty and precision, with such appropriateness, that they please the spirit and persuade it to take up its abode in them. This it does in special ceremonies, which the priest combines with sacrifices and invocations; at the climax of the ritual the presence of the divine spirit makes itself felt to the worshipper with the greatest immediacy and intensity.

The ancestor figure is the medium of the great progenitor, the quintessence of the tribal soul, for

Africans believe that the vital force of their ancestors continues to operate after death. Mother figures, for instance, ensure numerous progeny and fertility; but in Africa they have a different meaning from those of the Christian world. With us it is the divine child who supplies the central theme, whereas in Africa everything centres around the mother, who gives promise of offspring and bestows fecundity.

The large tribal figures are hidden from non-initiates in a secret place and are looked after by the priest. On important occasions they are carried to the place where the rite is performed, lavishly adorned, propitiated by sacrificial gifts and asked for their advice, which the spirit manifests to the priest through an oracle. Smaller tutelary figures and fetishes containing magic substances are considered personal property of every individual and occupy a special place in his hut. These, too, receive offerings at regular intervals.

The mask usually bears the features of the ancestor figure, but serves a different function: it is a dynamic ritual implement, which intervenes actively in the ceremonies. Its significance can only be appreciated by one who has seen it perform this function: in the light of the moon and the torches the mask-bearer appears, fully costumed, and suggests the presence of the great spirit by wild leaps and dances, speaking with an unnatural voice. Indeed, the mask-bearer is convinced that during his trance, in an atmosphere heightened by odours of sacrifice and the rhythmic beating of drums, he is possessed by the divine spirit, which pulsates through his body like an electric current.

The mask-bearer symbolizes, too, the protective power of the men's (rarely women's) secret society, a power which the society exercises over the village, and whose aid is invoked when danger threatens: in time of fire and drought, in war, illness and death. With its masks the secret society exorcises devils and witches who are deemed responsible for such evils. Without this mask, however, and without the suggestive rites, the dancers would have neither the courage nor the power to withstand the demonic forces — especially the souls of the dead, which are particularly feared since they are thought to be filled with jealousy and thirst for revenge against the living. For this reason spectacular masked dances and invocations are staged at funerals of leading members of the society.

Kindly souls appear in white masks, sometimes even dancing on stilts to look as supernatural as possible. With piping voices they announce the counsel given to the bereaved from the divinity. Festivals connected with the sowing of crops and harvesting, legal proceedings, ceremonies held for boys completing the bush school — on all important occasions the tutelary spirits are invoked and acclaimed. Every ritual act, every ceremony performed by the priest, gives the African a sense of security and an assurance that each evil spirit is counteracted by a kindly one.

All ritual implements, and also many utensils, are decorated with symbols and signs of the tutelary powers, so that the owner is constantly linked to the vital force. This is why we find in Africa such a wealth of beautifully decorated implements: ceremonial staffs, sceptres and thrones, harps and drums, as well as cups, bowls, spoons and pulley-holders for looms.

Form

Turning now to the creator of these objects, a question comes to mind: how does the African artist work? How does the wood-carver comply with ancient tribal traditions and find a form that is appropriate to the object's ritual function and worthy to serve as a receptacle for the vital force?

Unlike the Greeks, who extolled gods created in their own image (or even African courtly art, which attempted to reproduce visual reality), the classic Black artist consciously departs from the naturalistic image. By abstraction or by intensifying the natural features he attempts to create an entirely new form, as unreal as possible. In doing so he avails himself of all those elements which to him suggest power, which he sees in those beings endowed by the creator-god with extraordinary vital force: the great ancestor, the priest, the tribal hero, the mother, the young beauty. In fashioning them he confers upon them features which manifest their particular functions. An unusual degree of spiritual power is expressed by a large head with a bulging forehead; prestige and power, by the attributes of mighty animals.

Stereometric forms are also drawn upon to render vigour: jagged lines, notches, edges, bold curves suggest energy, or the shadows of the deep. The artist is very well acquainted with the whole range of means of expression.

The African artist allows wide scope to his fantasy in the mask, designed to embody the imaginary tutelary spirit and to give the impression of weird and ghostly movement. With colours, feathers and horns he accomplishes some astonishingly lively effects. In a slow creative process he brings to life a work which constitutes a new unit, a new being. If the sculpture proves to be a success, a helpful medium, the tribe adheres to this form and passes it on from generation to generation according to all the rules of the cult. Thus we have a style, a firmly established formal canon, which may not lightly be discarded, although certain nuances are permissible. For this reason a style retains its specific character for decades, even centuries. It stands and falls with the faith to which it is linked.

African art as such has been accredited with a quality of static austerity and restraint. But this does not prevent it from astonishing us with a vast range of potentialities and overwhelming us with its capacity for ever-fresh inspiration and skilful combinations. We find all the intermediary stages between the extremes of geometric abstraction and realistic expressiveness, from a delightful primitivism (Fon) to the most sophisticated refinement (Guro).

In geometric-oriented styles stereometric elements are

employed with angular, rounded, smooth and structured forms, and account is taken of light and shade effects.

In these works, most of them abstract, the artists have succeeded in making supernatural forces particularly apparent (Dogon, Mama, Bakwele, Waja, Ijo and Basonge).

The opposite tendency — the organic, realistic style — appeals to our emotions. It is closer to the model's natural anatomy. But while it respects the organic form of the original, it uses exaggerations to express the unreal quality of a supernatural being: over-emphasis of the head, eyes and hands; meticulously delineated lips, eyelids, eyebrows and cheeks; gradual transitions from one anatomical element to another. In the polyphonic concert that is African art (Senufo, Dan, Bajokwe, Mitsogho, Balega, Baluba), this style contributes the most poetic and moving notes.

In both trends we find the same basic principles:

extreme simplification of the figure and meticulous execution of such details as ornaments and colours. Especially beautiful is the bronze-like finish, which covers the sculpture's surface with a lustrous patina.

The African artist has an innate sense for rhythm and harmony of form, and he is able to lend vitality to his carving by using highly eccentric proportions. But even when he exaggerates natural features he does not let himself be carried away to the point of arbitrariness, but follows the formal canon, the proportions considered correct for the purpose of a particular work. Whether we call this feeling for proportion spiritual or not, the artist succeeds in conveying the essential elements by ignoring natural proportions. Therefore he deliberately carves a head that is extremely large or miniscule but not of normal size.

Depending upon the style employed, torso and limbs are either elongated (Ibo, Senufo) or else short and plump. The feet are frequently either hardly outlined or exaggerated, in order to accentuate the sense of stability. Sometimes they form one piece with the pedestal, sometimes they are omitted altogether.

The Artist

In Africa, as elsewhere in the world, the quality of a work is ultimately determined by the personal talent of the artist, which alone can elevate it above mediocrity. The most accomplished African artists are those who remain faithful to tribal traditions, for so long as they remain true to the ancient beliefs, they bring to their work the necessary intensity and experience. Besides these artists — especially within the orbit of the royal courts — there are a number of professional carvers who specialise in producing certain utensils for the market. With their work there is a considerable risk of it lapsing into routine and schematisation. Minor nuances determine whether a form is significant or not, whether abstraction bestows on it a high degree of intensity or remains an empty exercise. These nuances are responsible for the harmonious composition of the forms and determine whether it is a work of art or not. With the finest pieces the light gently outlines the simplified forms of the surface, and the contours merge with captivating elegance (Guro, Baluba).

In each style art can develop in a personal manner; in each, one may identify the talent of a sensitive master, for the African is quite capable of appreciating a masterpiece and of paying due respect and esteem to the artist. The artist draws upon the experiences, the mythological resources and the traditions of the community to which he belongs. He endeavours to emulate his great predecessors, but although he has to move within the framework of the formal canon, he attempts, by subtle nuances and variations, to produce ever finer and more effective works, which will be appreciated by his people and approved of by the great ancestor and tutelary spirit. As an artist in the ancient tribal tradition, he has the exalting feeling of modelling the tutelary forces, and he employs all the artistic and spiritual power of which he is capable. Fasting and sexual continence prepare him for his task. To undertake his carving, he withdraws from the gaze of unauthorised onlookers, and works to the accompaniment of offerings and songs, for contact with the realm of spirits is full of danger. Proud, yet conscious of his responsibility toward his tribe, the artist works with the utmost concentration and devotion. He goes about his task with patience, perseverance and masterly skill, aiming blows rapidly and accurately at the wooden block with his adze, until the final form emerges. For detailed work he uses the blade of the adze, which he wields like a knife. Many carvers leave it at that; others polish the surface with abrasive leaves or splinters of stone, dip the sculptures in a mud-bath, or treat them with some kind of coloured sap, oil, soot or resin.

Wood is the most popular material, and this is no coincidence, since the imposing trunk of an old tree is regarded by Africans as the bearer and guardian of magic powers.

Wood, however, has the disadvantage that it is quickly

worn out by ritual use and by the damp climate, or falls victim to the ravages of termites. This is why most of the works which we are familiar with and admire were carved during the last two hundred years. Whatever was created prior to this must be considered a regrettable loss. We can read about these works in ancient Arab chronicles, which tell of ancestor figures, masks and ritual dances in Black Africa.

Development and Dissemination of African Art

The origins of African art are enshrouded in the mists of history and are no longer ascertainable. The riches that we see today are the last link in a long, uninterrupted chain of artistic creations. Some archaeological finds in terracotta, stone and metal indicate the high level of accomplishment reached at a very early date. This is especially true of the Nok terracottas, for which radiocarbon dating gives the period between the fourth century B.C. and the second century A.D.

The great variety of styles is to a large extent the result of Africa's turbulent history, of the numerous migrations which have shattered this continent since time immemorial. Peoples of different race and colour have continually moved across the wide, open Sudanese steppes, traversed the Sahara by way of the ancient routes, and then followed the lakes and rivers to establish their settlements in the fertile savannah and in jungle clearings. These immigrants brought to their new homeland their own culture, techniques, commodities and religious beliefs; much was adopted by the indigenous tribes and incorporated into their own culture. Large and small kingdoms were founded, which flourished and declined. Wise kings with broad-minded views took the place of despotic rulers; conquerors, exploiters, slave-merchants brought unrest to the African peoples and caused entire tribes to flee into the jungle. Tribal feuds and headhunting disturbed their peaceful existence. But as a constant force there remained the village community, headed by its chief and council of elders — where, indeed, some secret society did not exercise power in an authoritarian manner in the name of the spirits.

So far as art is concerned, these chequered historical events brought about great enrichment so long as they were peaceful. New impulses and ideas moulded and modified the African peoples' ancient concept of the world. On the other hand, much was destroyed by militant conquerors, especially by the iconoclastic followers of Islam, and by various "prophets" who succeeded in persuading hundreds of thousands of people to support their new tutelary spirit or fetish, and whose zeal caused them to burn many ancient sculptures.

The changes which were most significant for Black Africa began in the Nile valley. Certain peoples traversed the Interlacustrine area and made their way to south-eastern Africa or followed the Ubangi river as far as the Congo basin. Others moved westwards across the central Sudan, either to Lake Chad and Nigeria or via the western Sudan to Sierra Leone. It was along these routes that, especially during the first millennium A.D., the iron culture found its way into Black Africa, together with many ideas from the ancient Orient, above all the institution of sacral kingship, which led to the foundation of the most important kingdoms. These were ruled by an absolute monarch who was worshipped as an incarnation of God upon earth. A whole series of strange customs and a specific type of ornamentation — plaited band and loops — appeared in these kingdoms; there is ample evidence pointing to inspiration from the Kushite kingdom on the middle reaches of the Nile (Napata and Meroë), which for its part had inherited cultural elements from ancient Egypt.

The art of the sacral kingdoms is entirely opposed to ancient tribal art. It is based upon a different artistic consciousness and on an entirely different artistic drive. The inspiration does not stem from the supernatural world but is terrestrial and completely oriented to human concerns. The artist summoned to the royal capital was charged with erecting a monument to the sacrosanct ruler, with fashioning his idealised portrait in precious and durable materials and decorated it with the royal insignia. The king monopolized for himself materials such as gold and bronze, precious stones and elephant's tusks, which were rare or difficult to obtain. It is to these sacred kings that we owe the splendid bronzes and terracottas of Ife and Benin, which show the amazing sense of observation, marked sensitivity and fine aesthetic sense of African artists.

The king and aristocracy demanded from the artist elaborate execution and lavish ornamentation of regalia; his achievements were acknowledged and remunerated in royal fashion. In this way the courts contributed to giving art a powerful stimulus.

In following the principal styles in African art from north to south, we at once notice that the artistic centres are concentrated in the western part of the continent and in the Congo area. No doubt the reason for this lies largely in historical events: the numerous migrations of earlier and later times, the wars and local feuds, and the clashes between various forms of religious belief. These factors created a complex situation which can no longer be unravelled. A tribal sculpture in the ancient tradition is to be encountered only among Black Africans, not among the Hamitic pastoral people of the steppes, although they, too, are dark-skinned, nor among the Pygmies of the jungle. Not even the Sudanese and Bantu, who live in what seem to be similar environmental conditions, employ cult figures.

Presumably the Muslim iconoclasts were chiefly responsible for the destruction of ancient tribal art. In western Sudan, on the other hand, the Muslims of the larger localities were unable to persuade the peasants of the environs to abandon their ancient customs, whose ritual required the use of masks and figures. Interestingly enough, the chief area where abstract-geometric sculpture flourished is located precisely in western Sudan. The sculptures of the Dogon and Bambara, famous for their austere grandeur, are sometimes simplified to the point of becoming symbolic signs. But among the Dogon there are also some very old figures — the *tellem* — which are distinctly naturalistic and expressive. A speciality of the Bambara is the elegant ritual mask in the shape of an antelope, the *chi wara*, fascinating in its countless variations. Among their neighbours, the Senufo and Lobi, we find masterpieces of the realistically rendered human figure. The masks of the Bobo, Mossi and Gurunsi combine vitality with decorative sense. In the states along the Atlantic coast, from Senegal to the Congo (Zaire), one style follows hard upon the heels of another. The vigorous geometric style of the Baga in Guinea displays clear traces of its derivation from the austere school of western Sudan.

Elsewhere, on the other hand, geometric style and naturalism are juxtaposed, as is the case with the Dan and Kran, the Ijo or the Ibo. In Sierra Leone there are archaeological finds in stone of extreme realism which testify to the existence of former kingdoms (Bulom and Sherbro), as well as to more recent tribal wood-carvings that have developed to the present day. The Baule and Guro from the Ivory Coast are excellent wood-carvers: they decorate with elaborate precision and care even the smallest ritual implements and profane objects as well, many of which manifest a highly developed aesthetic sensibility. The village fetishes of the Fon in Dahomey, on the other hand, are treated in such a naïve and little-differentiated way that we are inclined to call this primitive art.

In Nigeria we find numerous styles in both the geometric and realistic trend; also, by a stroke of good luck, bronzes, terracottas and ivory carvings from the flourishing periods of early courtly art have been discovered and preserved there. Precious objects of captivating beauty were produced in the courtly art of Ife and Benin and their offshoot in the lower Niger area. In the Cameroons there are kings who to this day reside in domed palaces lavishly decorated with carvings, and whose power is reflected in bold, dynamic and expressive sculptures. The Pangwe of the Gaboon chose expressive organic forms for their reliquary heads and figures. For the same purpose the Mahongwe, Bakota and others use completely abstract wooden plaques, ornamented with layers of copper and brass foil. The objects produced by the Bakwele are captivating in their severe abstraction; those of the Mitsogho and Bapunu in their delicate sensitivity.

In the vast area of the Congo outstanding styles are produced in the savannah areas bordering on the jungle along several tributaries of the Congo River. Most of them adhere to the naturalistic style, especially the sculptures of the Bakongo, Bajokwe and Baluba. Here one senses something of the splendour of the early kingdoms: the extreme sensitivity and spiritualisation of the Baluba and Bena-Lulua, the expressive realism of the Bajokwe and Bakongo, or the markedly decorative ability of the Bakuba. In the eastern part of the Congo area the tendency to abstraction increases in a striking way.

Among the Bantu of east and south-eastern Africa we find only sparse traces of tribal art. Finally, in Madagascar it was almost exclusively the Black tribes that produced carvings of any significance.

Our tour of Africa is over. Our hope is to have awakened the reader's curiosity and convinced him that in Black Africa we encounter an art whose best works are fully worthy to be placed alongside those of the West.

ILLUSTRATIONS

4

6

15

26

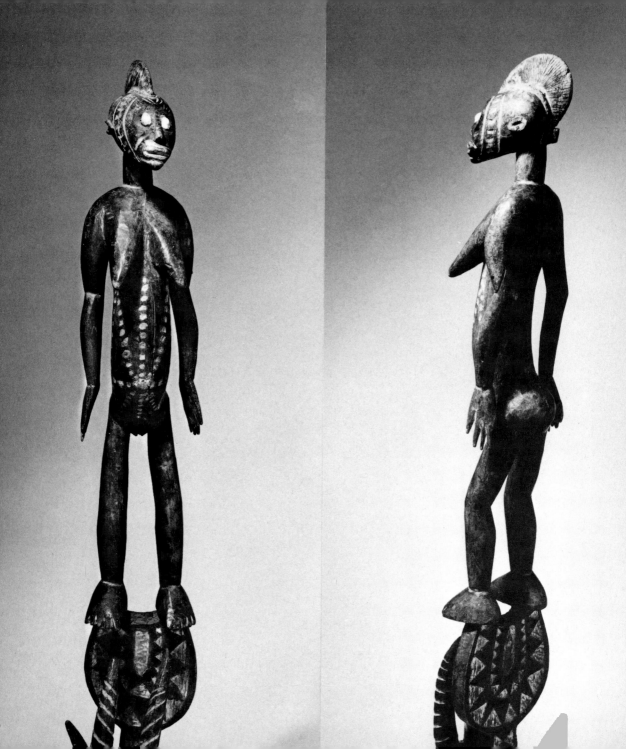

34

42

43

45

53

56

70

72

73

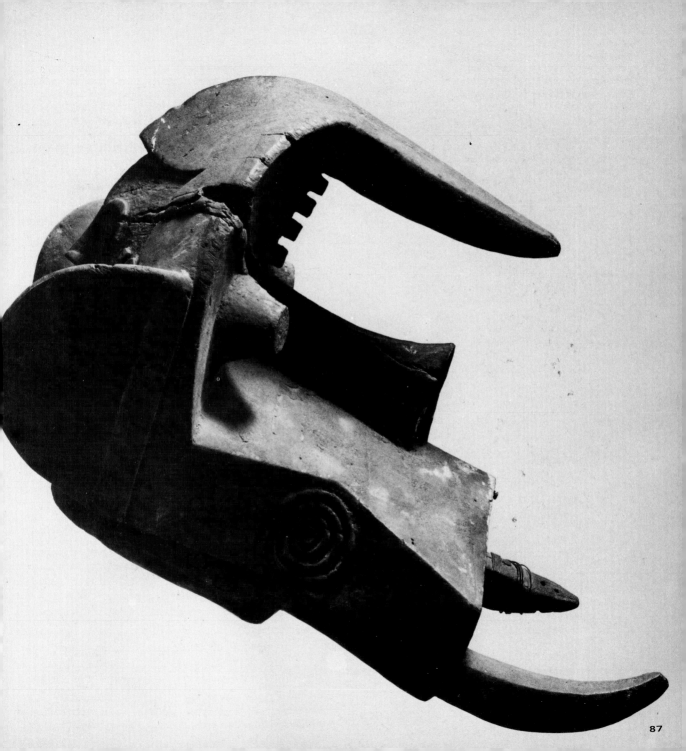

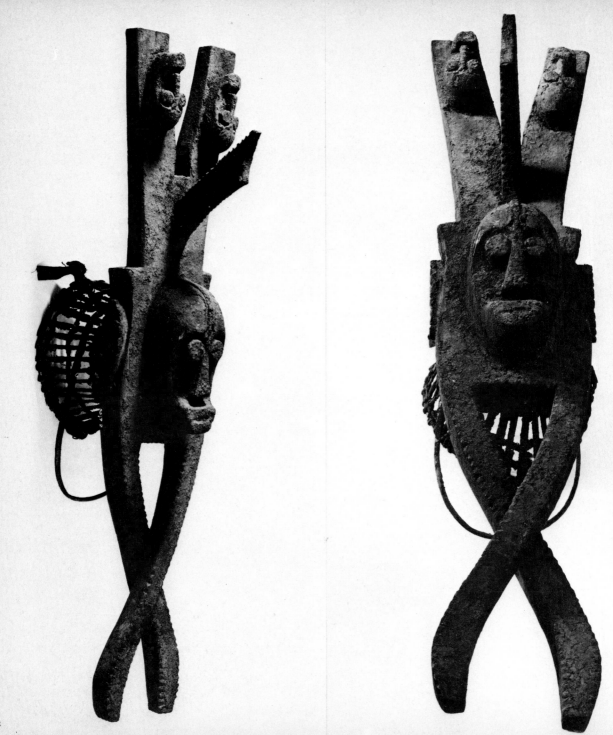

89

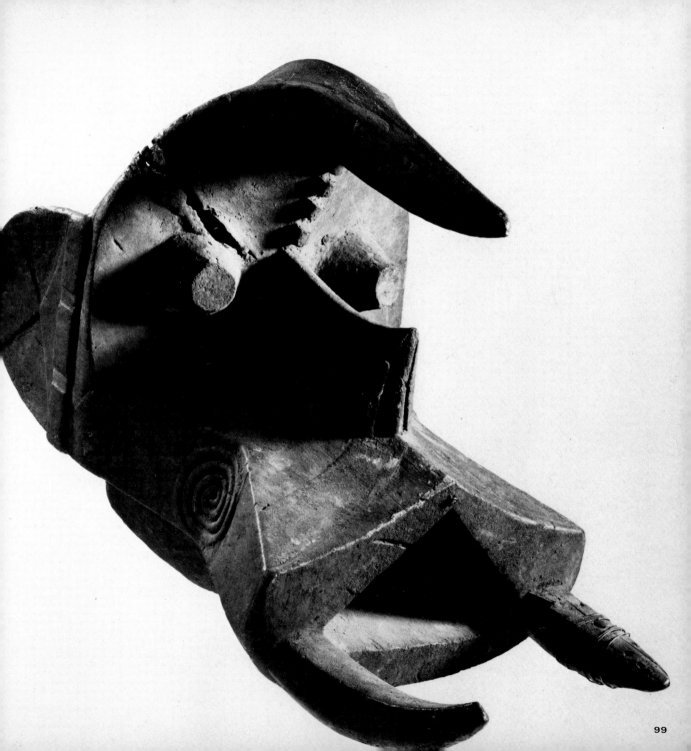

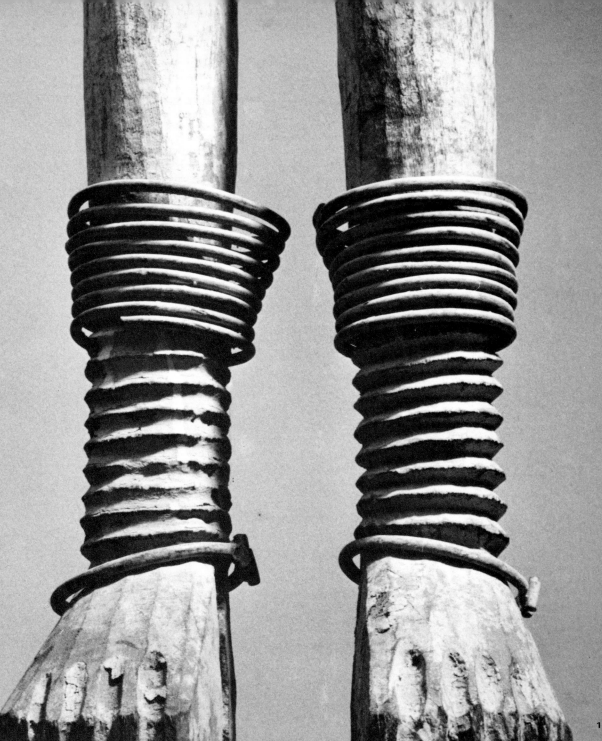

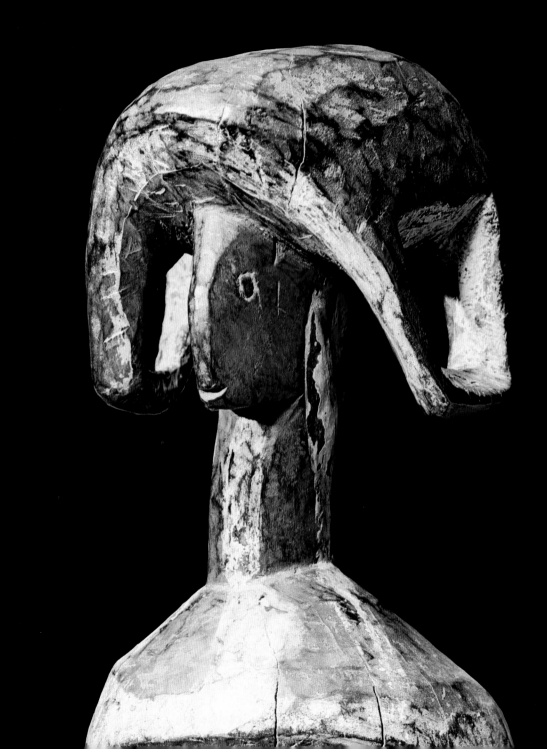

167

184

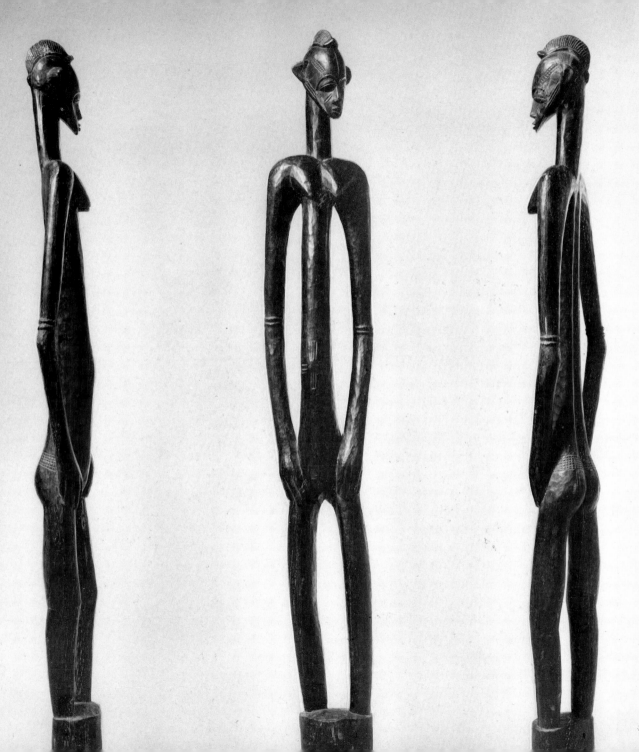

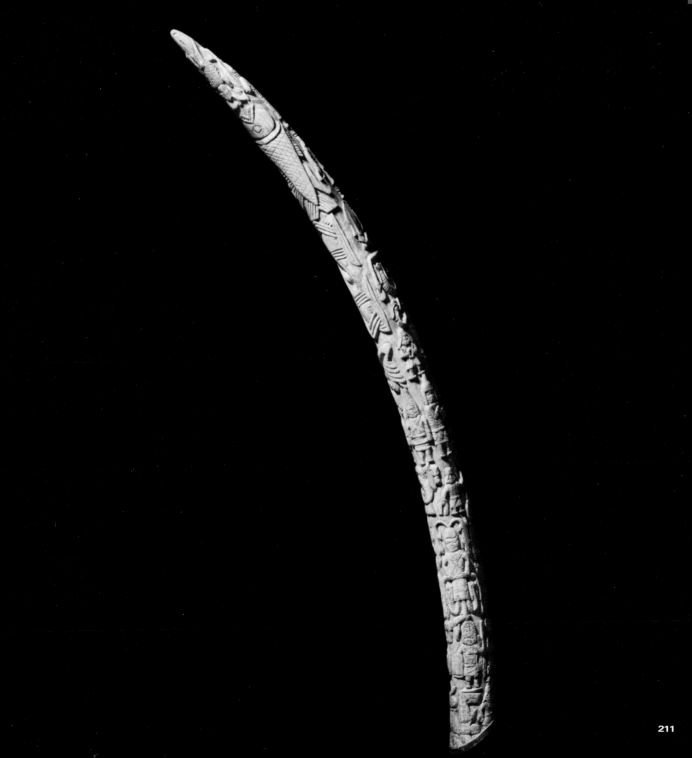

211

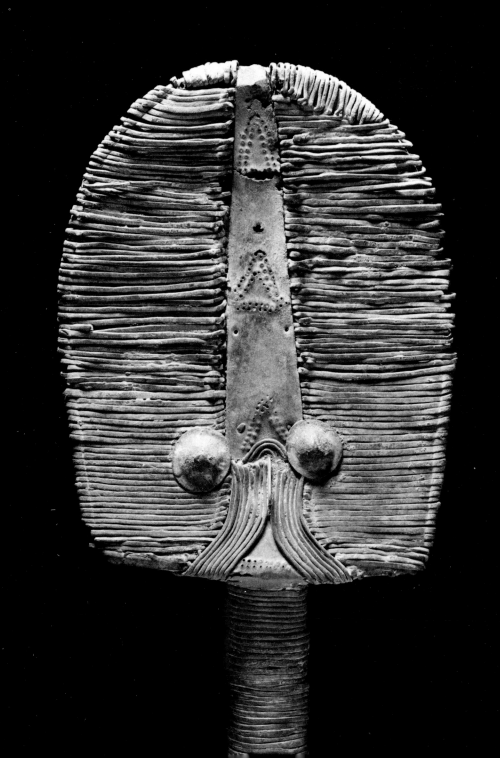

223

227

233

239

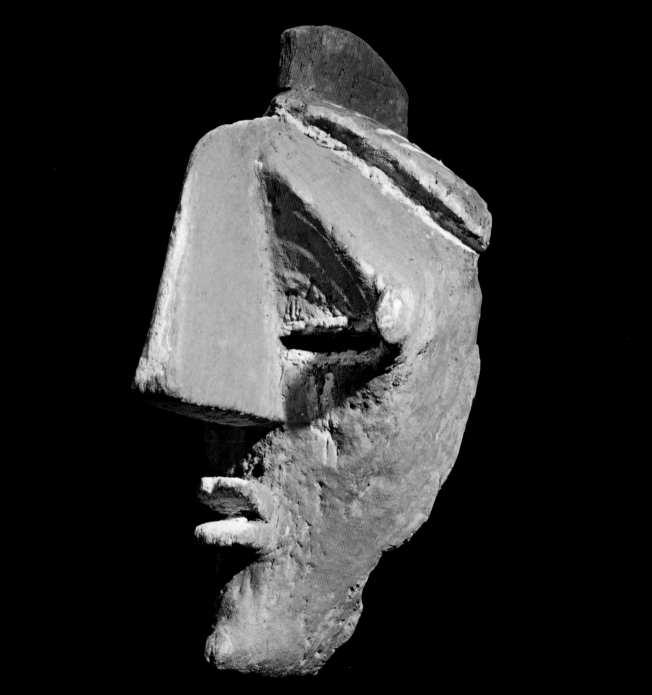

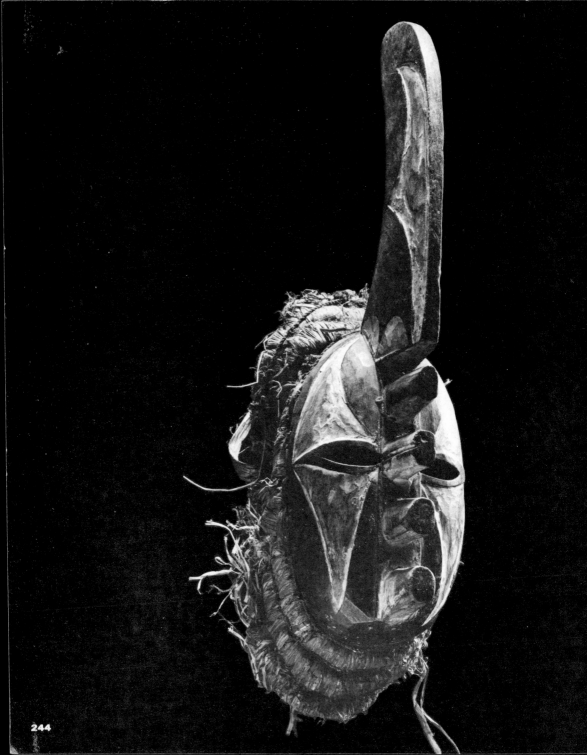

INDEX OF ILLUSTRATIONS

1. Face of the commemorative head of a priest-king. Bronze, 25 cm. Nigeria, Ife; 10th-13th century. Federal Department of Antiquities, Lagos, Nigeria. (See Plates 12, 49 & 240.)

2. Face of a head with ritual tattooing on the cheeks. Terracotta, 12.5 cm. Nigeria, Ife; 10th-13th century. Discovered by Bernard Fagg in 1953 under the shrine of Olokun Walode, the goddess of wealth. Federal Department of Antiquities, Lagos, Nigeria. (See Plates 10 & 224.)

3. Secret society mask. Wood, cane framework covered with raffia and painted bast, 54 cm. South-western Zaire, Bayaka. Rietberg Museum, Zurich.

4. Head with small top-knot. Terracotta, 20 cm. Ghana, Ashanti, Fomena style; 19th century. Discovered in a tomb; commemorative heads of the king or of the queen mother used to be placed in the necropolis as offerings. Dr. Ernst Anspach Collection, New York. (See Plate 70.)

5. Commemorative head of a king. Bronze, 1 mm. thick, with copper inlay on the forehead, 21 cm. Nigeria, Benin; early period, 1475-1525. Bronzes of the early Benin period are distinguished by the extreme thinness of the metal used. Peter Schnell Collection, Zurich.

6. Detail of the Tsoede bird. Brass, 140 cm. Nigeria, Tada village on the Middle Niger. This piece, exceptionally large for an object in cast metal, belongs to a group of ritual figures traditionally supposed to have been brought from Idah by Tsoede, the founder of the Nupe kingdom, during the 15th-16th centuries. Federal Department of Antiquities, Lagos, Nigeria. (See Plate 304.)

7. Bird with her young and serpent. Wood, 65 cm. Guinea, Baga. Used in the rice ceremonies. René Rasmussen Collection, Paris. (See Plate 208.)

8. Handle of a staff in the shape of an ibis. Bronze, 31 cm. Nigeria, Benin; 17th-18th century. A. Schwarz Collection, Amsterdam. (See Plate 209.)

9. Animal's head used as a dance head-dress. Wood covered with skin, 86 cm. South-eastern Nigeria, Cross River Region, Ekoi. Maurice Nicaud Collection, Paris.

10. Head with tattooing. (See Plates 2 & 224.)

11. Back view of the head in Plate 4, showing the whorls of the top-knot.

12. The head in Plate 1, with its diadem. (See Plates 1, 49 & 240.)

13. Commemorative head of a queen mother, with pointed cap adorned with beads. Bronze, 3 mm. thick; height 35 cm. Nigeria, Benin; 16th century, early period. City of Liverpool Museums, Liverpool. (See Plate 229.)

14. Head of a hippopotamus with diadem. Terracotta, 12.5 cm. Nigeria, Ife-Lafogido; 10th-13th century. Found

by Professor Ekpo Eyo in 1969. Federal Department of Antiquities, Lagos, Nigeria.

15 & 16. Plaque in relief depicting a girl. Bronze, 31 cm. Nigeria, Benin, Great period; late 16th-early 17th century. The body is decorated with scarification and the leopard on her hand is a symbol of power. Ornamental background of rosettes. A Schwarz Collection, Amsterdam.

17. Figure on horseback. Bronze, 56 cm. Nigeria, Benin; Middle (Great) period. 17th-mid-18th century. It represents a rider, with plumed crown, armour and trappings, come from Northern Nigeria to visit the court of Benin. The head belongs to the British Museum, London, while the rest of the body is in the Sammlung für Völkerkunde, Zurich.

18. Figure bedecked with jewels. Brass, 30.5 cm. Nigeria, Katsena-Ala, Tiv. Maurice Bonnefoy Collection, D'Arcy Galleries, Geneva.

19. Female votive figure. Brass, 30.5 cm. Eastern Nigeria, Jalingo region. Maurice Bonnefoy Collection, D'Arcy Galleries, Geneva.

20. **Degele** or helmet-mask. Wood, 92 cm. Northern Ivory Coast, Korhogo district, Lataha village, Senufo. These masks, worn by the highest dignitaries of the Ló secret society, are seen in pairs at nocturnal funeral ceremonies. The cock's-comb coiffure is an evocation of the sacred bird of the soul; the arms are lacking. Rietberg Museum, Zurich. (See Plates 82, 83, 84 & 140.)

21. Side view of the piece in Plate 17.

22. Statuette. Weathered wood 27 cm. Eastern Nigeria, Mambila. Pierre Harter Collection, Paris.

23. Nail fetish. Wood and iron nails, 45 cm. Dahomey, Fon. Comte Baudouin de Grunne Collection, Wezembeek-Oppem, Belgium. (See side view in Plate 238.)

24 & 25. Sceptre with two-faced head and royal head-dress. Wood, 46 cm. Angola, Bajokwe. André Fourquet Collection, Paris.

26, 27 & 28. Figure of a king with asymmetrical hands. The **tshihongo** coiffure is a symbol of command. Museum of the Philadelphia Civic Center, Philadelphia.

29. Female figure representing an ancestress with child. Wood with reddish patina, 75 cm. Mali, Dogon, **tellem** style. Maurice Nicaud Collection, Paris. (See detail in Plate 182.)

30 & 31. Antelope mask crowned with a female figure. Wood, painted red and white, 109 cm. Upper Volta, Mossi. The Wango secret society used these masks at funerals and to protect the fruit of their trees. Rietberg Museum, Zurich.

32. **Mba** mask with seated figure. Wood, 51 cm. Nigeria, Ibo. This mask was used in the Iko Okochi ceremonies of the yam harvest. Alfred Muller Collection, St. Gratien, France.

33. Mask of the Mmwo secret society. Painted wood, 46 cm. Nigeria, Onitsha region, Ibo. Used for invoking the spirit of a dead woman. Manchester Museum, Manchester. (See side view in Plate 232.)

34. Mask with bird. Wood, 40 cm. Ivory Coast, Baule. Private collection, Paris.

35. Cup in the shape of a head with ram's horns. Wood, 20 cm. Central Zaire, Bakuba. The ram's horns are a symbol of power, while the ornamental scarifications are the distinctive of the family. Sammlung für Völkerkunde, Zurich.

36. Secret society mask with leopard. Painted wood and raffia, 45 cm. Used in the concluding ceremonies of the bush school for boys. South-western Zaire, Bayaka. Erdrich Collection, Sammlung für Völkerkunde, Zurich.

37. Weaver's pulley-holder with male head. Wood, 22 cm. Ivory Coast, Baule. With the pulley fitted into its base, this piece was used to guide the warp. Pierre Verité Collection, Paris.

38. Head of a looking-glass fetish. Wood and glass, 22 cm. Western Zaire, Bakongo. Elsy Leuzinger Collection, Zurich. (See Plates 151, 196 & 197.)

39 to 43. Equestrian group. Polychrome wood, 37 cm. Nigeria, Yoruba; 17th century. This group, carved in Nigeria, was presented to the king of Ketu in Dahomey. M. et Mme. Bellier Collection, Paris.

44. Fragment of an **oshe shango** or ritual club. Wood, 60 cm. Nigeria, Yoruba. This club, in the form of a priestess with a double axe, was used to invoke Shango, the god of thunder. Jacques Kerchache Collection, Paris. (See Plate 85.)

45 & 46. Ancestor figure. Wood, 79.4 cm. Eastern Zaire, Kabambara territory, Eastern Baluba tribe, Babuye. This figure represents King Adessa, grandson of the conqueror. Museum of Primitive Art, New York. (See Plates 48 & 188.)

47. Cult figure with geometrical head. Wood, 130 cm. Eastern Nigeria, Waja. Jacques Kerchache Collection, Paris. (See Plate 69.)

48. Detail from Plates 45 & 46. (See Plate 188.)

49. Another view of the face of the commemorative head in Plates 1, 12 & 240.

50. **Kifwebe** mask. Wood with traces of white paint, 35 cm. Central Zaire, Bakuba. Geometrical in form, with stylized linear composition. Rietberg Museum, Zurich. (See Plate 53.)

51 & 52. Detail of the little head crowning a ceremonial axe. Wood, copper and iron, 36.5 cm. South-eastern Zaire, Baluba. Emblem of chieftainship. Executed in a curvilinear style. Rietberg Museum, Zurich.

53. **Kifwebe** mask. Wood painted white and red, 60 cm. Central Zaire, Besonge. Used after sacrificing a slave as a protection against wars or epidemics. Rietberg Museum, Zurich.

174. The **bochio** in Plate 117.
175. Figure from the gable of a house, representing a mother with her child. Weathered wood with traces of red paint, 82 cm. South-western Zaire, Bapende. M. et Mme. Delenne Collection, Brussels. (See Plate 183.)
176. Ancestor statue. Weathered wood, 145 cm. Cameroon grasslands, Bamileke. The male figure, slightly inclined, wears a demon's head in his head-dress and holds a sword-hilt in his hand. Private collection, Geneva. (See detail in Plate 142.)
177. Initiation mask of a Mbuya musician. Painted wood and bast, 52 cm. South-western Zaire, Bapende. The beard symbolizes a powerful tutelary spirit. Kongo-Kwango Museum, Heverlee, Belgium.
178. Buffalo mask. Wood painted red, white and black, 75 cm. Upper Volta, Bobo. This mask personified the tutelary spirit of Dó and carried out a police function by driving evil spirits away from funerals and the rites preceding work in the fields. Rietberg Museum, Zurich.
179. **Chi wara**, antelope dance head-dress. Wood, 64 cm. Mali, Bambara, Minianka type. It represents a doe with her fawn on her back. Pierre Verité Collection, Paris. (See Plate 204.)
180. Another view of the two-faced head in Plate 179.
181. Little terracotta head, 23 cm. Northern Nigeria, Nok culture. Datable between 400 B.C. and 200 A.D. Fragment of a clay figure found by Bernard Fagg in 1943. Federal Department of Antiquities, Lagos, Nigeria.
182. Detail of the piece in Plate 29.
183. Another view of the figure in Plate 175.
184. Pair of ancestor figures. (See Plates 167 & 168.)
185. Seated figure. Weathered wood, 55 cm. Cameroon grasslands, Bekom. Pierre Harter Collection, Paris.
186. The same **Degele** figure as in Plates 82, 83 & 84.
187. **Po** spoon with human head. Wood, bast and kaolin, 63.5 cm. North-western Ivory Coast, Dan. With this spoon the **wunkirle** (most hospitable woman) scooped out the rice at banquets. Maurice Bonnefoy Collection, D'Arcy Galleries, Geneva.
188. The same figure as in Plates 45, 46 & 48.
189. The same **Ekwotame** figure as in Plate 79.
190 to 192. Throne supported by a kneeling woman. (See Plates 96 & 97.)
193. The same cup as in Plates 35 & 100.
194. Weaver's pulley-holder with braid and beard. Wood, 19.5 cm. Ivory Coast, Baule. The pulley fitted into its base to guide the warp. Walter Kaiser Collection, Stuttgart.
195. Ancestor figure. Wood, 88 cm. South-eastern Zaire, Baluba. Etnographisch Museum, Antwerp, Belgium.
196 & 197. Looking-glass fetish. (See Plates 38 & 151.)

198 & 199. Looking-glass fetish. Wood, glass and other materials, 23 cm. Western Zaire, Bakongo-Basundi. These fetishes, with the head and the body filled with magic substances, were handed out by witch-doctors as tutelary images. Rietberg Museum, Zurich.
200. Detail of the throne of the Sultana of Ukerewe. Wood, 107 cm. East Africa, Wanyamwezi. Museum für Völkerkunde, Berlin. (See Plate 202.)
201. **Deble**, or rhythm figure. Blackened wood, 108 cm. Northern Ivory Coast, Senufo. At funeral ceremonies and in the rites of initiation into the Ló secret society, these figures were used by the candidates to beat the ground rhythmically, invoking fertility. Elsy Leuzinger Collection, Zurich. (See detail in Plate 74.)
202. Throne of the Sultana of Ukerewe. (See Plate 200.)
203. Horseman. Iron, 15 cm. Northern Ivory Coast, Senufo. Emil Storrer Collection, Zurich.
204. On the left, **Chi wara**. (See Plate 179.) On the right, Tsoede bird. (See Plate 6.)
205. Sculpture of a bull. Iron, 24 cm. Tanzania, Bukoba. Linden-Museum für Völkerkunde, Stuttgart.
206. Antelope mask. Wood with geometrical figures painted in black, grey and blue, 110 cm. Upper Volta, Bobo-Fing. Maurice Nicaud Collection, Paris.
207. Animal mask. Painted wood, 39 cm. Eastern Nigeria, Mambila. Jacques Kerchache Collection, Paris.
208. The same bird as in Plate 7.
209. The same as in Plate 8.
210. Detail of the following plate.
211 to 213. Elephant's tusk carved in relief. Ivory, 169 cm. Nigeria, Benin; 19th century. It represents kings with their retinues, several Portuguese, animals and other symbols. One of the kings, Oba Oseñ, who is represented with mud-fish for legs and a serpent belt, was worshipped as the incarnation of the sea-god Olokun. Edith Hafter Collection, Zurich.
214. Figure of a priest. Encrusted wood, 45 cm. Mali, Dogon, Tellem style. The head ornament is the symbol of the **hogon** or priest; the arms are raised in a prayer for rain. Rietberg Museum, Zurich. (See Plate 243.)
215. Detail of a double gong. Ivory, 36 cm. Nigeria, Benin; 16th century, early period. Two little figures are seated on the upper edge. Background filled with an interlaced geometrical motif. Acquired in 1897 when Britain conquered Benin. A. Schwarz Collection, Amsterdam.
216. **Guli** mask in the form of a wild boar. Wood, 119 cm. Ivory Coast, Baule. Musée des Arts Africains et Océaniens, Paris. (See Plate 218.)
217. Side view of an **Igbile** head-dress in the form of a head. Painted wood, 54 cm. Nigeria, port of Ughoton, Bini, western Ijo style. This geometrical head was carved in 1897 as a protection against the

British punitive expedition. Igbile is the river spirit. Brian Egerton Collection, Ringwood, Hants., England. (See Plates 220 & 231.)
218. Another view of the **Guli** mask in Plate 216.
219. The same piece as in Plate 133.
220. **Igbile** (See Plates 217 & 231.)
221. Dance mask of the Ngil secret society. Wood, 50 cm. Gaboon, Fang. Pierre Verité Collection, Paris.
222. **Mbulu-ngulu**, guardian figure. Wood, copper and brass foil, 25 cm. Congo-Brazzaville, Bakota. These figures were placed on top of receptacles containing the skulls and bones of village founders and other tribal heroes. Jacques Kerchache Collection, Paris.
223. **Bweti**, guardian figure. Wood and metal plates, 24 x 26 cm. Gaboon, Mahongwe. The **Bweti** were fastened to baskets containing the bones of the most important members of the tribe. Jacques Kerchache Collection, Paris.
224. Head with tattooing on the cheeks. (See Plates 2 & 10.)
225. **Bweti**, guardian figure. Wood and metal plates, 26 cm. Jacques Kerchache Collection, Paris.
226. Highly stylized mask encircled by two horns. Wood, 55 cm. Gaboon-Congo-Brazzaville, Bakwele. Charles Ratton Collection, Paris.
227. **Mboto-mboli** helmet mask. (See Plate 106.)
228. Side view of a mask with very prominent facial features: Painted wood, 26 cm. North-western Ivory Coast, Ngere. Max and Berthe Kofler-Erni Collection, Basle. (See Plate 230.)
229. The same commemorative head as in Plate 13.
230. Mask with very prominent facial features. (See Plate 228.)
231. Detail from Plates 217 & 220.
232. Side view of the mask in Plate 33.
233. Rear face of the double mask in Plates 87, 99 & 130.
234. Mask of the Bwame secret society. Wood and white kaolin, 14 cm. North-eastern Zaire, Balega. Emblem of very high rank. W. and D. Alder Collection, Rothrist, Switzerland.
235. Mask. Wood and brass foil, 36 cm. Völkerkunde-Museum, Zurich.
236. Very abstract mask. Wood, 49 cm. Mali, Dogon. Jacques Kerchache Collection, Paris.
237. Gelede mask. (See Plates 98 & 103.)
238. Side view of the fetish in Plate 23.
239. **Maji** masks. Painted wood, 43 and 33 cm. Nigeria, Ibo. Used in the yam ceremonies. Jacques Kerchache Collection, Paris. (See Plate 244.)
240. Commemorative head of a priest-king. (See Plates 1, 12 & 49.)
241. Male initiation mask. Wood painted red and white, 32 cm. Southern Zaire, Balwalwa. Musée Royal de l'Afrique Centrale, Tervuren, Belgium.
242. Painted bark cloth similar to the one in Plate 147.
243. Detail from Plate 214.
244. **Maji** mask. (See Plate 239.)

zembeek - Oppem, Belgium. (See Plate 115.)

114. The same figure as in Plate 112.

115. Head of the ancestor figure in Plate 113.

116. **Bochio,** village fetish. Wood, 176 cm. Dahomey. **Bochios** are tutelary spirits of the cult of the god Legba. Jacques Kerchache Collection, Paris.

117. Fragment of a double-headed **bochio,** or village fetish. Wood, 43 cm. Dahomey, Fon. Jacques Kerchache Collection, Paris. (See Plate 174.)

118 & 119. Kneeling figure with five heads. Wood, 32 cm. Mali, Dogon. René Rasmussen Collection, Paris. (See Plate 121.)

120. The 1970 Exhibition of the Art of Black Africa at the Kunsthaus, Zurich. Bambara sculptures in wood from Mali. Ancestor figures, tops of antelope masks, antelope staff and (on the wall) mask of N'tomo, the tutelary spirit of the uncircumcised boys' society.

121. Different views of the piece in Plates 118 and 119.

122. Pair of **Debles,** or rhythm figures. Wood, 95 and 108 cm. Northern Ivory Coast, Korhogo district, Lataha village, Senufo tribe. At funeral ceremonies and rites of initiation into the Ló secret society, candidates struck the ground with these figures in vigorous rhythm, to invoke fertility. The female figure is in the Rietberg Museum, Zurich and the male figure is in the Museum of Primitive Art, New York. (See detail in Plate 138.)

123. The 1970 Exhibition of the Art of Black Africa at the Kunsthaus, Zurich. Figures in wood of the Senufo (Northern Ivory Coast) and, in the right foreground, of the Lobi (Upper Volta).

124 & 125. The same Exhibition Hall as in the preceding plate. From left to right: pair of **Degele** helmet-masks; **Deble** rhythm figure; double mask of Waniugo, the tutelary spirit of the Ló secret society.

126 & 127. The 1970 Exhibition of the Art of Black Africa at the Kunsthaus, Zurich. Figures in wood from Nigeria. In the foreground, Ibo ancestor figures. In the background, from left to right: Beni-Ijo helmet-mask; Ibo dance head-dress; Igala masks; Waja ritual figure.

128. Figures in wood from Nigeria. In the foreground, Ibo ancestor figures. In the background, from left to right: Ibo dance head-dress; two Bini dance head-dresses in the Ijo style; Ibo head-dress; hippopotamus water-spirit mask of the Kalabari-Ijo; Ibo geometrical double mask; Igala mask.

129. Feet of an Ibo figure, Nigeria.

130. Side view of Plates 87 & 99.

131. Large mask. Pale wood, 67 cm. Cameroon grasslands, western Bamileke. This much-feared mask symbolized the executive power of the king and was borne before him on all official occasions. Rietberg Museum, Zurich.

132. Ritual dagger. Brass, iron, wood and leather, 49.5 cm. Central Zaire, Bakuba. The iron blade has incised decoration. Maurice Bonnefoy Collection, D'Arcy Galleries, Geneva.

133. Dance mask. Wood painted red, black and white, 130 cm. Border region between southern Upper Volta and west central Ghana; Gurunsi. This flat mask with buffalo horns is of the male type. Galerie Simone de Monbrison, Paris.

134 & 135. The 1970 Exhibition of the Art of Black Africa at the Kunsthaus, Zurich. Art of the Bambara and Minianka (Mali), of the Bobo (Upper Volta) and of the Gurunsi-Abron (Upper Volta-Ghana). From left to right: Bambara sculptures; centre, Gurunsi-Abron dance mask, Bobo mask, Tussian mask (Banfora area), two Minianka terracotta figures.

136. Prisoner with his hands tied behind his back. Wood, 77 cm. Upper Volta, Lobi. Jacques Kerchache Collection, Paris. (See Plates 148 & 149.)

137. Hermaphrodite. Wood with traces of red paint, 100 cm. Western Zaire, lower reaches of the river Kwilu, Bayanzi. This figure, which is known as **mpuwu,** has ornamental scarification on the face and is the tutelary figure of the village. Musée Royal de l'Afrique Centrale, Tervuren, Belgium. (See Plate 139.)

138. Detail from Plate 122.

139. Detail from Plate 137.

140. **Degele,** top of a helmet-mask. (See Plates 20, 82, 83 & 84.)

141. Pair of **edan** figures. Brass and iron, 19.5 cm. The female figure is the one in Plate 108. The male figure is making the gesture of the Ogboni secret society. Both in the Theo Dobbelmann Collection, Amsterdam.

142. Detail of an ancestor figure. Weathered wood, 145 cm. Cameroon grasslands, Bamileke. Private collection, Geneva. (See Plate 176.)

143. Fragment of an ancestor figure. Badly weathered wood, 116 cm. Mali, Bambara. Hélène Kamer Collection, Paris.

144 & 145. Mother with child, in asymmetrical posture. Wood, 26.5 cm. Upper Volta, Lobi. Maurice Nicaud Collection, Paris.

146. Pair of ancestor figures. Polychrome wood, 160 and 151 cm. Nigeria, Ibo. They bear the same scarifications as the men of the tribe. Private collection, Geneva.

147. Painted bark cloth. 145 cm. Chad. Musée des Arts Africains et Océaniens, Paris. (See Plate 242.)

148 & 149. The same figure as in Plate 136.

150. Nail fetish. Wood, traces of white paint and iron nails, 77 cm. Western Zaire, Mayombe district, Bakongo. This threatening spirit, Nkonde, is invoked in acts of vengeance or of harmful magic. André Fourquet Collection, Paris.

151. Looking-glass fetish. Wood and glass, 22 cm. Western Zaire, Bakongo. The small receptacle on the

woman's back is filled with magic substances. Elsy Leuzinger Collection, Zurich. (See Plates 38, 196 & 197.)

152. **Bieri,** reliquary head. Wood with traces of paint, 39 cm. Gaboon, Pangwe. Considered the seats of the soul of the tribe, the **bieri** were placed on top of bark boxes containing the skulls and bones of village founders and other tribal heroes. Rietberg Museum, Zurich. (See Plate 162.)

153. On the left, head of a harp. Wood and leather, 11 cm. (Total length of the harp, 98 cm.). North-Eastern Zaire, Mangbetu. On the right, harp with double-headed figure. Wood and leather, 55 cm. North-eastern Zaire. The narrow head, artificially deformed, is characteristic of the court culture of the Mangbetu. Both in the Rietberg Museum, Zurich.

154 & 155. Details of the heads in the preceding plates.

156 & 157. The 1970 Exhibition of the Art of Black Africa at the Kunsthaus, Zurich. Ancestor figures of the Mumuye, eastern Nigeria.

158. Detail of an ancestor figure with loop ornamentation. Wood, 127 cm. Eastern Nigeria, Mumuye. René Salanon Collection, Paris. (See Plate 161.)

159. Ancestor figure. Wood, 100 cm. Eastern Nigeria, Mumuye. Tiny rhomboidal head. Jacques Kerchache Collection, Paris.

160. Female ancestor figure. Wood, 92 cm. Eastern Nigeria, Mumuye. Comte Baudouin de Grunne Collection, Wezembeek-Oppem, Belgium.

161. Another view of the figure in Plate 158.

162. The **bieri,** or reliquary head, in Plate 152.

163. **Bieri,** reliquary figure. Wood, 25.5 cm. Gaboon, Pangwe. André Fourquet Collection, Paris.

164 & 165. Cult figure with expressive face. Weathered wood, 121 cm. Nigeria, Waja. René Salanon Collection, Paris.

166. Head. Weathered wood, 50 cm. Mali, Tellem style. Ornamental scarifications on the cheeks. Jacques Kerchache Collection, Paris.

167 & 168. Pair of ancestor figures. Weathered wood, 80 cm. Southern Madagascar. They belonged to an Aloala grave. Jacques Kerchache Collection, Paris. (See Plate 184.)

169 & 170. Two seated figures playing the balafon. Wood, 44 cm. Mali, Dogon. Tellem style. Hélène Kamer Collection, Paris.

171. Harp with female figure. Wood painted white, 80 cm. Southern Gaboon, Mitsogho. Galerie Simone de Monbrison, Paris.

172. Statuette with expressionistic hands. Iron, 19.5 cm. Central Zaire, Bakuba. Etnographisch Museum, Antwerp, Belgium.

173. Female figure with child. Weathered wood, 116 cm. Madagascar, Negro tribes in the south of the island. R. Duperrier Collection, Paris.

54 & 55. Double mask. Wood, 28 cm. Ivory Coast, Baule. Pierre Verité Collection, Paris.

56. Mask crowned with four animal figures Wood, 42 cm. Cameroon grasslands, Mamileke. Galerie Künzi, Oberdorf-Solothurn, Switzerland.

57. Mask with round eyes and beard. Wood with dark, lustrous patina, 24 cm. Western Ivory Coast, Dan. This mask is used by initiates of the Poro secret society to represent the great mother spirit of their tribe; the man wearing it walks on stilts to the accompaniment of softly-playing wind instruments. This spirit settles disputes and protects new-born children and boys in the bush school. René Rasmussen Collection, Paris.

58. Mask of the sacred bush cow. Wood, 38 cm. Northern Nigeria, Afo. Elsy Leuzinger and J. Neukom-Tschudi Collection, Federal Department of Antiquities, Lagos, Nigeria.

59. Mask with half-closed eyes and bell ornaments. Wood painted red, metal and bast, 27 cm. North-western Ivory Coast, Dan-Ngere. Alfred Muller Collection St. Gratien, France.

60. **Kpelie** double mask. Wood, 25 cm. Northern Ivory Coast, Senufo. Emil Storrer Collection, Zurich.

61. Mask with ornamental scarification. Wood, 31.5 cm. Ivory Coast, Baule, Yaure type. Rietberg Museum, Zurich.

62 to 64. Epa mask with horseman. Wood, 110 cm. Nigeria, Yoruba. The masks of the Epa secret society represented the spirits of the dead. Federal Department of Antiquities, Lagos, Nigeria. (See Plate 78.)

65. Ritual vessel. Bronze, 11.5 cm. Nigeria, Ita Yemoo, Ife, 10th-13th century. It bears the representation of a queen, wearing a diadem and holding a sceptre in her hand, the figure winding round a pot that stands on a throne, while the handle rests on a stool. Federal Department of Antiquities, Lagos, Nigeria. (See Plate 76.)

66. Detail of a seated figure with bulbous coiffure. Soapstone, 70 cm. Nigeria, Esie. Federal Department of Antiquities, Lagos, Nigeria. (See Plate 110.)

67. Top of a **Nimba** head-dress. Wood, 109 cm. Guinea, Baga. Nimba is the most powerful of the tutelary spirits of the Simo secret society. It appears at funerals and during the rice harvesting and threshing ceremonies. The man wearing this head-dress is concealed under a raffia costume and looks out through a hole between the breasts. Rietberg Museum, Zurich.

68. **Nimba** dance head-dress. Wood, 128 cm. Guinea, Baga. Symbol of fertility. Max and Berthe Kofler-Erni Collection, Zurich.

69. Detail of Plate 47.

70. Side view of the piece in Plate 4.

71. Head of a weaver's pulley-holder. Wood, 12 cm. Ivory Coast, Guro. ·

The pulley fitted into the base was used to guide the warp. Rietberg Museum, Zurich.

72 & 73. Mahan Yafe, spirit of the chieftain of a tribe. Stone, 23 cm. Northern Sierra Leone, 13th-15th century. An archaelogical find, highly venerated by the natives. Max and Berthe Kofler-Erni Collection, Basle.

74. Detail of a **Deble** or rhythm figure. Blackened wood, 108 cm. Northern Ivory Coast, Senufo. Elsy Leuzinger Collection, Zurich. (See Plate 201.)

75. Commemorative statue of King Kwete Peshanga Kena. Wood, 72 cm. Central Zaire, Bakuba. Early 20th century. Ethnographical Department, Danish National Museum, Copenhagen.

76. Another view of Plate 65.

77. Detail of the figure in Plate 75.

78. Figure of horseman from the Epa mask in Plates 62, 63 & 64.

79. **Ekwotame** figure. Wood, 63 cm. Nigeria, Idoma. This figure of a mother seated on a throne, with her child on her back, was placed beside the head of a deceased king. Philip Goldman Collection, Gallery 43, London.

80 & 81. Bowl with a kneeling woman. Wood, 23 cm. Nigeria, Yoruba. The nuts for the Ifa oracle were kept and presented in such bowls. Rietberg Museum, Zurich.

82 to 84. Pair of **Degele**, or helmet-masks topped with figures. Wood, 99 and 92 cm. Northern Ivory Coast, Korhogo district, Lataha village, Senufo. These masks, which indicate the highest rank in the Ló secret society, appear in pairs at nocturnal funeral ceremonies. The poisoned arrows in the male figure's quiver may symbolize shafts of lightning. Both figures wear cock's-comb coiffures evoking the sacred bird of the soul; the arms are lacking. Rietberg Museum, Zurich.

85. Top of an **oshe shango** ritual club, front view. (See Plate 44.)

86. Buffalo mask. Wood painted a reddish colour, 48 cm. Northern Nigeria, Mama. This magnificently stylized mask was worn for funeral ceremonies and sacrifices. Federal Department of Antiquities, Lagos, Nigeria.

87. Double mask. Wood, 30 cm. Nigeria, Ibo. Main face: blend of geometrical, human and animal elements; the animal's mouth with fangs. Rear face: a human countenance. René Salanon Collection, Paris. (See Plates 99, 130 & 233.)

88. Mask of the water spirit. Wood and bark, 65 cm. Nigeria, Ijo; early 20th century. This mask represents the water spirit Sapele with his children. Federal Department of Antiquities, Lagos, Nigeria.

89. Throne of beads forming a serpent motif. Wood, coloured beads and cowries, 130 cm. Cameroon grasslands. Presented to the Grand Duke of Baden by Sultan Njoya at the beginning of the 20th century. Rautenstrauch-Joest Museum, Cologne.

90. One leaf of the double doors from a barn, with ancestor figures in relief. Wood, 62 cm. Mali, Dogon. Rietberg Museum. Zurich.

91. Pair of ancestor figures. Wood, 66 cm. Mali, Dogon. Rietberg Museum, Zurich.

92 to 95. Drum with kneeling woman. Wood, 114 cm. Guinea, Baga. Private collection, Paris.

96 & 97. Detail of a throne supported by a kneeling woman. Wood, 53 cm. South-eastern Zaire, Baluba. A work by the artist known as the Master of Buli. Linden-Museum für Völkerkunde, Stuttgart. (See Plates 190, 191 & 192.)

98. Face of a Gelede mask. Painted wood, 27 cm. Dahomey, Yoruba. These masks of the Gelede secret society appear during the sowing rites to invoke fertility. Private collection, Geneva. (See Plates 103 & 237.)

99. Main face of the double mask in Plates 87, 130 & 233.

100. Detail of the cup in Plates 35 & 193.

101. Gelede mask adorned with loops. Wood, 34 cm. Dahomey, Yoruba. Used by the Gelede secret society during the sowing rites to invoke fertility. W. and D. Alder Collection, Rothrist, Switzerland.

102. Two-faced head. Wood, copper nails and kaolin, painted, 26 cm. Southern Gaboon, Mitsogho. André Fourquet Collection, Paris. (See Plate 180.)

103. Gelede mask, front view. (See Plates 98 & 237.)

104 & 105. Mother and child. Wood, 35.6 cm. Southern Zaire, Bena-Lulua; 19th century. Tutelary figure. The Brooklyn Museum, New York.

106. **Mboto-mboli** helmet mask. Painted wood, 70 cm. Gaboon, Ivindo region, Bakota. Used in initiation ceremonies. Christian Duponcheel Collection, Tervuren, Belgium. (See Plate 227.)

107. **Mwana pwo,** girl's mask. Painted wood, bast and metal rings, 28 cm. Southern Zaire, Bajokwe; 19th century E. Deletaille Collection, Brussels.

108. Female figure of the Ogboni secret society. Brass and iron, 19.5 cm. Nigeria, Yoruba. Theo Dobbelmann Collection, Amsterdam. (See Plate 141.)

109. Ancestor figure. Wood painted red, 139 cm. Nigeria, Ibo. Jacques Kerchache Collection, Paris.

110. Seated figure. Soapstone, 70 cm. Federal Department of Antiquities, Lagos, Nigeria. (See Plate 66.)

111. Head crowning a post. Wood with traces of paint, 71 cm. Upper Volta, Lobi. Jacques Kerchache Collection, Paris.

112. Ancestor figure. Painted wood, 136 cm. Nigeria, Ibo. Jacques Kerchache Collection, Paris. (See Plate 114.)

113. Ancestor figure. Painted wood, 174 cm. Nigeria, Ibo. Comte Baudouin de Grunne Collection, We-